I0439825

A Wedding Guide for New Pastors

Pastor Patti Chiappa

'A Wedding Guide for New Pastors'

By

Pastor Patricia Chiappa

Copyright 2015

All rights Reversed. No part of this book may be reproduced , stored in a retrieval system, or transmitted in any way or by any means. Electronic, mechanical, photocopy or otherwise without written permission of the writer.

2

Prelude

Performing a wedding is a blessing bestowed upon you by Almighty God himself. It is a precious gift not only to the bride and groom and their families but to you. Anyone asked to perform a wedding should not take the duties of performing a wedding lightly, because you play a very special part in making the day as memorable as possible.

As a new minster, you may feel nervous or overwhelmed about being asked to officiate your first wedding, but this guide will walk you through the most important steps of a Christian Wedding, Or a Renewal Ceremony. This guide is a step by step easy to read guide that any new pastor can follow. So relax, enjoy and remember you play a part in making a special memory for the bride and groom.

"Processional- Chapter 1"

The processional is the start of the wedding ceremony and it involves the presentation of the bridal party and eventually the bride. During the processional, which is usually set to music, first the bridal party walks down the aisle, and is then followed by the bride. The general protocol for the processional allows first for the seating of parents, then bridesmaids walk down the aisle accompanied by groomsmen. Next, the maid of honor follows, then the flower girl and ring bearer (if used), and then the bride enters and makes her way down the aisle.

Some moving songs to suggest to the bride and groom to use for their processional is as follows:

Traditional/Classic

1. "Air" (from Water Music Suite), (George F. Handel)

2. "Bridal Chorus" (from Lohengrin), (Richard Wagner)

3. "Canon in D" (Johann Pachelbel)

4. "Procession of Joy" (Hal Hopson)

5. "Rigaudon" (Andre Campra)

6. "Spring" (from The Four Seasons), (Antonio Vivaldi)

7. "Te Deum" (Marc-Antoine Charpentier)

8. "The Prince of Denmark's March" (Jeremiah Clarke)

9. "Trumpet Tune" (Henry Purcell)

10. "Trumpet Voluntary" (Jeremiah Clarke)

11. "Trumpet Voluntary" (John Stanley)

12. "Wedding March" (from The Marriage of Figaro), (Wolfgang Amadeus Mozart)

Traditional Alternatives

13. "Canzon V" (Giovanni Gabrieli)

14. "Coronation March for Czar Alexander III" (Peter J. Tchaikovsky)

15. "Overture" (from Royal Fireworks Music), (George Frederic Handel)

16. "Promenade" (from Pictures at an Exhibition), (Modest Mussorgsky)

17. "Romeo and Juliet Love Theme" (Tchaikovsky)

18. "Sinfonia" (from Cantata No. 156), (Johann S. Bach)

19. "Toccata" (from L'Orfeo), (Claudio Monteverdi)

20. "Trumpet Tune in A-Major" (David N. Johnson)

21. "Sonatas for Organ, Op. 65, No. 3 (con moto maestoso)," (Felix Mendelssohn)

22. "Winter," Largo, (from The Four Seasons), (Antonio Vivaldi)

Contemporary

23. "Appalachia Waltz" (Yo-Yo Ma, Edgar Meyer, Mark O'Connor)

24. "Sunrise, Sunset" (from Fiddler on the Roof), (Sheldon Harnick & Jerry Bock)

25. "The Look of Love" (Dionne Warwick/Burt Bacharach)

26. "The Vow" (Jeremy Lubbock)

27. "To A Wild Rose" (Edward MacDowell)

28. "Flatbush Waltz" (Andy Statman)

29. "Wedding Processional" (from The Sound of Music), (Richard Rodgers & Oscar Hammerstein)

Religious/Sacred

30. "All People That On Earth Do Dwell" ("Old 100th" hymn)

31. "Dona Nobis Pacem" (16th century hymn)

32. "Hanava Babanot" (A Love Song), (Neeman)

33. "St. Anthony's Chorale" (Franz Joseph Haydn)

34. "Hymn Fanfare from The Triumphant" (Francois Couperin)

35. "Scalero de Oro" (traditional Sephardic)

"Greetings- Chapter 2"

At this point in the wedding, the pastor will be asked to extend a greeting to the wedding guests. This is a standard greeting I use for all couples.

Dearly beloved, we are gathered here in God's presence to witness and to celebrate the marriage of Groom's name _____ and Bride's name_____, and to ask God to bless them so that they may be strengthened for their life together. We are called to rejoice in their happiness, and find in their love a reason to renew our own commitments to those whom are near and dear to each of us. God gave us marriage for the full expression of love between a man and a woman so that husband and wife may cherish and delight in one another; comfort and help each other in sickness, trouble and sorrow; provide for each other in temporal things; pray for and encourage each other in the things that pertain to God; and live together faithfully all the length of their days.

"Opening Prayers- Chapter 3"

An Opening prayer should not only welcoming the bride and groom warmly, but also the wedding guests.

You may want to use one the following introductions to not only greet the bride and groom but also all of the wedding guests.

To the Bride and groom please choose what opening prayer you would like to use in your wedding by circling one of these examples.

Sample Opening Prayer #1

Our Father, love has been your richest and greatest gift to the world. Love between a man and woman which matures into marriage is one of your most beautiful types of loves. Today we celebrate that love. May your blessing be on this wedding service? Protect, guide, and bless ____ and ____ in their marriage.

Surround them and us with your love now and always. Amen.

Sample Opening Prayer #2

Heavenly Father, ___ and ___ are now about to vow their unending loyalty to each other. We ask you to accept the shared treasure of their life together, which they now create and offer to you. Grant them everything they need, that they may increase in their knowledge of you throughout their life together. In the name of Jesus. Amen.

Sample Opening Prayer #3

God, for the joy of this occasion we thank you. For the significance of this wedding day we thank you. For this important moment in an ever growing relationship we thank you. For your presence here and now and for your presence at all times, we thank you. In Christ's holy name. Amen.

The Pastor will then ask " Who gives this bride away?"

The person walking the bride down the aisle should then response " I/We do."

At this time a Hymn or Song can be played.

Bride and Groom please indicate here if you will be playing a song or hymn at this time by circling (Yes/ No)

Some song examples are as follows:

Amazing Grace- A Classical Hymn

Partial Hymn Lyrics:

The Lord has promised well to me,

His word my hope secures;

He will my shield and portion be,

As long as life endures.

Love Divine, All Love Excelling- Wedding Hymn All About Love

Partial Music Lyrics:

Love divine, all loves excelling,

Joy of heaven to earth come down;

Fix in us thy humble dwelling;

All thy faithful mercies crown!

Jesus, Thou art all compassion,

Pure unbounded love Thou art;

Visit us with Thy salvation;

Enter every trembling heart.

Abide with Me- God Leading the Marriage

Partial Hymn Lyrics:

I need Thy presence every passing hour.

What but Thy grace can foil the tempter's power?

Who, like thyself, my guide and stay can be?

Through cloud and sunshine, Lord, abide with me

How Great Though Art- Glory To God

Partial Song Lyrics

Then sings my soul, My Savior God, to Thee,

How great Thou art, how great Thou art.

Then sings my soul, My Savior God, to Thee,

How great Thou art, how great Thou art!

All Things Bright and Beautiful- Simply A Beautiful Hymn

Partial Hymn Lyrics:

God gave us eyes to see them,

And lips that we might tell

How great is God Almighty,

Who has made all things well?

O Perfect Love- A Love Song

Partial Hymn Lyrics:

O perfect Love, all human thought transcending,

Lowly we kneel in prayer before Thy throne,

That theirs may be the love which knows no ending,

Whom thou forevermore dots join in one.

Be Thou My Vision- God is our vision

Be Thou my Vision, O Lord of my heart;

Naught be all else to me, save that Thou art.

Thou my best Thought, by day or by night,

Waking or sleeping, Thy presence my light.

All Creatures of Our God and King- A Wonderful Hymn Choice

Partial Hymn Lyrics:

All creatures of our God and King

Lift up your voice and with us sing,

Alleluia! Alleluia!

Thou burning sun with golden beam,

Thou silver moon with softer gleam!

These eight choices would all make a great Christian Wedding hymn for any ceremony.

"Statement of Intention- Chapter 4"

The statement of intention tells all who attend the wedding that the bride and groom desire to be married out of their own free will. The pastor may use these statements for the Bride and Groom's free will Intention to marry. To the bride and groom this is a standard one I use for all weddings.

Today is the day that _ (Add groom name here) _____ and   bride's name here) _____will formally and publicly make their promises to one another. Although this is indeed a high point, marriage is a journey not a destination. Marriage is more than any one single event or promise. It is a series of decisions that have been made, and will continue to be made over and over again, every day, that shows each of their care and concern for the one whom they each love most in the world.

Marriage is a promise that is renewed daily through a couples actions and a responsibility taken on in the spirit of faith, and hope, and love, that brings comfort in times of sadness and heightens our greatest joy.

(Declaration of Intent)

(Groom's name) _____ and (bride's name) _____.may the promises you make this day live always in your hearts and in your home so that all which you share now deepen and grow through the years, leading you through a lifetime of happiness.

A wedding is more than a celebration of the Love which lives in our Bride and Groom's hearts today. It reaches into the future and proclaims their intentions for that which tomorrow shall hold. A couple who wed are joined not only by the mutual affection and love they share, but also by their hopes, dreams and by their promises of what will be... The promises and vows they make this day shall guide them into their common future. I will ask you now if you are prepared to make these promises.

"Wedding Vows- Chapter 5"

Wedding Vows are the highlight of the ceremony. Each bride and groom will have an idea of what their wedding vows should be. Some couples may choose to write their own vows. Others may want a more traditional wedding and recite their vows with the help of a pastor.

Bride and Groom, please indicate Here if you are using your own or indicate sample number on this space:

If a couple chooses to write their own vows a pastor will choose to say: " The bride and groom have chosen to express their love in a very special way and they have written their own wedding vows. Let us come before God with love in our hearts and in prayerful silence , let us listen to the song of the bride and groom's heart as they express their love for one another."

If the bride and groom would like to go a more traditional route, here are some examples of vows that a pastor may use:

To Groom) Example One (Traditional)

_____, please take _____'s hand while I recite these vows.

Will you _____ offer yourself to _____ as your wife,

Your friend, your lover and your lifelong companion.

Will you share your life with hers; build your dreams together, support her through times of trouble,

And rejoice with her in times of happiness;

Will you treat her with respect, love and loyalty through all the trials and triumphs of your lives together?

This commitment is made in love, kept in faith, lived in hope, and eternally made new.

(Groom answers) I will

To Bride) Example One

_____, please take _____'s hand while I recite these vows.

Will you _____ offer yourself to _____ as your husband,

Your friend, your lover and your lifelong companion.

Will you share your life with his; build your dreams together, support him through times of trouble,

And rejoice with him in times of happiness;

Will you treat him with respect, love and loyalty through all the trials and triumphs of your lives together?

This commitment is made in love, kept in faith, lived in hope, and eternally made new.

(Bride Answers) I will

Groom (Example 2)

Non-Denomination Wedding Vow Sample 1

"I _____, take thee _____, to be my wife/husband.

To have and to hold,

In sickness and in health,

For richer or for poorer,

And I promise my love to you forevermore"

Non-Denomination Wedding Vow Sample 2

I _____, take you _____, to be my wife/husband.

To share the good times and hard times side by side.

I humbly give you my hand and my heart

As a sanctuary of warmth and peace,

And pledge my faith and love to you.

Just as this circle is without end, my love for you is eternal.

Just as it is made of incorruptible substance,

My commitment to you will never fail. With this ring, I thee wed."

Non-Denomination Wedding Vow Sample 3

Before our friends and those so special to us here,

On this wonderful day of gladness and good fortune,

I _____ take

You _____ as my wife/husband, in friendship and in

love,

In strength and weakness,

To share the good times and misfortune, in

Achievement and failure, to celebrate life with you

forevermore.

"First Readings- Chapter 6"

After the wedding vows are declared, many couples will use this point in their wedding ceremony to have someone read a scripture that is special to them.

Please indicate here Bride and Groom what reading you would like to use at this time and who will be reading it by sample numbers in this space: If no reading write None:

First Reading number:

Read By:

Frist Reading Choices: First Reading Scriptures from the Old Testament

Reading Number 1: Genesis 2:18-24 - The Second Creation Story

And the Lord God said, it is not good that the man should be alone; I will make him and help meet for him. And out of the ground the Lord God formed every beast of the field, and every fowl of the air; and brought them unto Adam to see what he would call them; and whatsoever Adam called every living creature, that was the name thereof. And Adam gave names to all cattle, and to the fowl of the air, and to every beast of the field; but for Adam there was not found a help meet for him. And the Lord God caused a deep sleep to fall upon Adam and he slept, and he took one of his ribs, and closed up the flesh instead thereof. And the rib, which the Lord God had taken from man, made him a woman, and brought her unto the man. And Adam said, this is now bone of my bones, and flesh of my flesh; she shall be called Woman, because she was taken out of Man. Therefore shall a man leave his father and his mother, and shall live with his wife and they shall be one.

Reading Number 2: Tobit 8, 4-8 Tobias prays for God's mercy for himself and Sarah on their wedding night

When the girl's parents left the bedroom and closed the door behind them, Tobias arose from bed and said to his wife, "My love, and get up. Let us pray and beg our Lord to have mercy on us and to grant us deliverance." She got up, and they started to pray and beg that deliverance might be theirs. He began with these words: "Blessed are you, O God of our fathers; praised be your name forever and ever. Let the heavens and all your creation praise you forever. You made Adam and you gave him his wife Eve to be his help and support; and from these two the human race descended. You said, 'It is not good for the man to be alone; let us make him a partner like himself.' Now, Lord, you know that I take this wife of mine not because of lust, but for a noble purpose. Call down your mercy on me and on her, and allow us to live together to a happy old age." They said together, "Amen, amen,"

Reading Number 3: Ruth 1:16-17 Where You Go I will Go

But Ruth said, "Entreat me not to leave you or to return from following you; for where you go I will go, and where you lodge I will lodge; your people shall be my people, and your God my God; where you die I will die, and there will I be buried. May the LORD do so to me and more also if even death parts me from you?"

Reading Number 4: Song of Songs 2:8-10, 14, 16; 8:6-7 - Solomon's Song

"Set me as a seal upon your heart, as a seal upon your arm; for love is strong as death, passion fierce as the grave. Its flashes are flashes of fire, a raging flame. Many waters cannot quench love, neither can floods drown it. If one offered for love all the wealth of one's house, it would be utterly scorned"

At this time a Musical Interlude may be chosen. Bride and Groom please indicate here if you will have a Musical Interlude or if I shall go right into the second reading:

Please indicate here Bride and Groom what reading you would like to use at this time and who will be reading it by sample numbers in this space: If no reading write None:

Second Reading number:

Read By:

Second Reading Scriptures from the New Testament

Reading Number 1: Ephesians 5:21-33 l Submitting To One Another

Submitting yourselves to one another in the fear of God. Wives, submit yourselves unto your own husbands, as unto the Lord. For the husband is the head of the wife, even as Christ is the head of the church; and he is the savior of the body. Therefore as the church is subject unto Christ, so let the wives be to their own husbands in everything.

Husbands, love your wives, even as Christ also loved the church, and gave himself for it. That he might sanctify and cleanse it with the washing of water by the word. That he might present it to himself a glorious church, not a having spot, or a wrinkle or any such thing; but that it should be holy and without blemish. So ought men to love their wives as their own bodies. He that loved his wife loved himself. For no man ever yet hated his own flesh; but nourished and cherished it, even as the Lord the church. For we are members of his body, of his flesh, and of his bones. For this cause shall a man leave his father and mother, and shall be joined unto his wife, and they two shall be one flesh. This is a great mystery, but I speak concerning Christ and the church. Nevertheless let every one of you in particular so love his wife even as he and the wife see that she reverence her husband.

Reading Number 2: Ecclesiastes 4:9-12 Two Are Better Than One

Two are better than one, because they have a good return for their toil. For if they fall, one will lift up his fellow; but woe to him who is alone when he falls and has not another to lift him up. Again, if two lie together, they are warm; but how can one be warm alone? And though a man might prevail against one who is alone, two will withstand him.

Reading number 3: 1 John 4:7-12 Love is From God;

Beloved, let us love one another, because love is from God; everyone who loves is born of God and knows God. Whoever does not love does not know God, for God is love. God's love was revealed among us in this way; God sent his only Son into the world so that we might live through him. In this is love, not that we loved God but that he loved us and sent his son to be the atoning sacrifice for our sins. Beloved, since God loved us so much, we also ought to love one another. No one has ever seen God; if we love one another, God lives in us, and his love is perfected in us.

Reading Number 4:1 Corinthians 12:31 - 13:8 The Qualities of Love "Love is patient; love is kind; love is not envious or boastful or arrogant or rude. It does not insist on its own way; it is not irritable or resentful; it does not rejoice in wrongdoing, but rejoices in the truth" (verses 4 - 6). 1 Corinthians 12 in the NAB; 1 Corinthians 13 in the NAB.

Bride and Groom at this time you can chose a Gospel reading or I can proceed into Charge to Family and Friends, Please Indicate here what you would like: Gospel reading/ Charge

Reading number 1: Mark 10:6-10 What God Has Joined Together

But at the beginning of creation God made them male and female. For this reason a man will leave his father and mother to be united to his wife, and the two will become one flesh. So they are no longer two, but one. Therefore what God has joined together, let man not separate.

Reading number 2: John 15 9:12 Jesus' Commandments

As the Father hath loved me, so have I loved you. Continue in my love. If ye keep my commandments, and abide in his love, even as I have kept my Father's commandments, and abide in his love. These things have I spoken unto you, that my joy might remain in you, and that your joy might be full. This is my commandment. That ye love one another as I have loved you.

Reading Number 3: 1 John 4:16-21 Rely on the Love of God

And so we know and rely on the love God has for us. God is love. Whoever lives in love lives in God, and

God in him? In this way, Love is made complete among us so that we will have confidence on the Day of Judgment, because in this world we are like him. There is no fear in love. But perfect love drives out fear, because fear has to do with punishment. The one how fears is not made perfect in love. We love because he first loved us. If anyone says, "I love God," yet hates his brother, he is a liar. For anyone who does not love his brother, whom he has seen, cannot love God, whom he has not seen. And he has given us this command: Whoever loves God must also love his brother.

Reading Number 4: John 3:18-24 Love With Action and Truth

Dear children, let us not love with words or tongue but with actions and in truth. This then is how we know that we belong to the truth, and how we set our hearts at rest in his presence whenever our hearts condemn us. For God is greater than our hearts, and he knows everything. Dear friends, if our hearts do not condemn us, we have confidence before God and receive from him anything we ask, because we obey his commands and do what pleases him. And this is his command; to believe in the name of his Son, Jesus Christ, and to love one another as he commanded us. Those who obey his commands live in him, and he in them. And this is how we know it by the Spirit he gave us.

Reading Number 5: John 2:1-11 The Wedding in Cana

On the third day there was a marriage at Cana in Galilee, and the mother of Jesus was there; Jesus also was invited to the marriage, with his disciples. When the wine failed, the mother of Jesus said to him, "They have no wine." And Jesus said to her, "O woman, what have you to do with me? My hour has not yet come." His mother said to the servants, "Do whatever he tells you." Now six stone jars were standing there, for the Jewish rites of purification, each holding twenty or thirty gallons. Jesus said to them, "Fill the jars with water." And they filled them up to the brim. He said to them, "Now draw some out, and take it to the steward of the feast." So they took it. When the steward of the feast tasted the water now become wine, and did not know where it came from (though the servants who had drawn the water knew), the steward of the feast called the bridegroom and said to him, "Every man serves the good wine first; and when men have drunk freely, then the poor wine; but you have kept the good wine until now." This, the first of his signs, Jesus did at Cana in Galilee, and manifested his glory; and his disciples believed in him.

If the bride and groom have not chosen a gospel reading then the pastor will say: Marriage is not something that two people invent, or construct by themselves. It takes a far wider community of family and friends to make any marriage work. Each of you have been invited here today because you are a part of that community. Therefore, having heard (Groom's name)_____ and Bride's name _____ state their intentions to each other and to God in this Service of Marriage, do you, pledge to support their union and to strengthen their lives together, to speak the truth to them in love, and with them to seek a life of love for others?

The people (or the congregation) shall answer: Yes, we do

"Exchange of rings- Chapter 7"

At this point in the wedding, it is time for the rings to be exchanged. The minster is to ask for the rings from the best man. Then the ring for bride shall be given to the Minister, who shall pass it to the groom, who shall then put it upon the bride's fourth finger, saying after the Minister:

Groom's name here:

Repeat after me:

This ring I give you; in token and pledge; of our constant faith; and abiding love. May the circle of our love be endless and our joys be measured in our hope in the Lord.

Then the ring for the groom shall be given to the Minister, who shall pass it to the bride, who shall then put it upon the groom's fourth finger, saying after the Minister:

Bride's name here:

Repeat after me:

This ring I give you: in token and pledge: of our constant faith: and abiding love. May the circle of our love be endless and our joys be measured in our hope in the Lord.

Then the pastor shall say: May the Lord of Love grant you a lifetime of blessings that flow from the stream of Heaven and from the savior's own loving heart. Let us pray.

Most merciful and gracious God, in whom we live and move and have our being, bestow upon these your servants the seal of your approval, and benediction; granting unto them grace to fulfill, with pure and steadfast affection, the vow and covenant between them made. Guide them together, we ask, in the way of justice and peace, that, loving and serving you, with one heart and mind, all the days of their life, they may be abundantly enriched with the tokens of your everlasting favor, in Jesus Christ our Lord. Amen.

"The Lord's Prayer- Chapter 8"

At this time the bride and Groom can either choose to have the pastor lead their wedding guests in the Lord's prayer or have a candle lighting or a rose ceremony

Bride and groom please indicate which one you chose here.

If the Bride and Groom Has chosen The Lord's Prayer the pastor will then say," Can we all unite our souls by holding the hand of the person next to us as we pray: Our Father who art in heaven, hallowed be thy name. Thy kingdom come. Thy will be done on earth as it is in heaven. Give us this day our daily bread, and forgive us our trespasses, as we forgive those who trespass against us, and lead us not into temptation, but deliver us from evil. For thine is the kingdom, and the power, and the glory, for ever and ever. Amen. –

If The Bride and Groom Has chosen a Unity Candle the Minster is to say; From every human being, there rises a light that reaches straight to heaven. And when two souls are destined to find each other, their two streams of light flow together and a single brighter light goes forth from their united being. They do not lose their individuality; yet, in marriage, they are united in so close a bond that they become one. Now, following the profession of their marriage vows, they will light the large center candle from the smaller candles to symbolize this new reality. In this way, they are saying that henceforth their light must shine together for each other, for their families, and for their community. At this time I invite the bride and groom to untie their lives as one.

If The Bride and Groom has chosen a rose ceremony the pastor will say: At this time the bride and groom want us to remember all the special angels that who are not here today but who have helped them on the road to finding each other. Both the bride and groom will place a red rose on the altar of their love to remember their love ones who now live in paradise with our Lord.Do not stand at my grave and forever weep. I am not there; I do not sleep. I am a thousand winds that blow. I am the diamond glints on snow. I am the sunlight on ripened grain. I am the gentle autumn's rain .When you awaken in the morning's hush. I am the swift uplifting rush, of quiet birds in circled flight. I am the soft stars that shine at night .Do not stand at my grave and forever cry. I am not there. I did not die. I rejoice in your love today, In your hearts I will always stay. Let us take a few moments in silence to remember them.

At this time the bride and groom may play a short two minute song to remember their loved ones.

Bride and Groom please indicate here if you have chosen some music   circle yes/ no

"Wedding Prayer / Closing prayer- Chapter 9"

This is the last prayer the minster is to say before the bride and groom kiss. This is the prayer I use at all weddings.

Let us pray.

Most merciful and gracious God, in whom we live and move and have our being, bestow upon these your servants the seal of your approval, and benediction; granting unto them grace to fulfill, with pure and steadfast affection, the vow and covenant between them made. Guide them together, we ask, in the way of justice and peace, that, loving and serving you, with one heart and mind, all the days of their life, they may be abundantly enriched with the tokens of your everlasting favor, in Jesus Christ our Lord. Amen. By the authority given unto me as a Minister in the Church of Christ, I declare that bride's name _____ and groom's name_____ are now Husband and Wife, according to the ordinance of God, and the law of the State; in the name of the Father, and of the Son, and of the Holy Spirit. Amen

Then causing the bride and the groom and to join right hands, the Minister shall say:

Therefore, what God has joined together, man must never separate." The grace of Christ attend you, and the love of God surround you, the Holy Spirit keep you, that you may live in faith, abound in hope, and grow in love, both now and forevermore. Amen.

Then the Minister shall say: You many kiss the bride.

Recessional

The recessional is the exact opposite of the processional. The bride and groom make their way down the aisle together, followed by the rest of the wedding party and their parents. The recessional marks the finish of the wedding ceremony. Congratulations! Now you're officially married. Congratulations! Pastors you have just preformed a wedding!

Please indicate here if you choose recessional music.

www.ingramcontent.com/pod-product-compliance
Lightning Source LLC
Chambersburg PA
CBHW080545290526
45790CB00006B/2561